CADMOS DOG TRAINING

The Invisible Link to Your Dog

CADMOS
DOG TRAINING

Read
Learn
Know

Angie Mienk

The Invisible Link to Your Dog

A new way of achieving harmony between dogs and humans

Copyright © 2011 Cadmos Publishing Ltd, Richmond Upon Thames, UK
Copyright of original edition © 2010 Cadmos Verlag GmbH, Schwarzenbek, Germany
Design: Ravenstein + Partner, Verden
Setting: Grafikdesign Weber, Bremen
Cover Photograph: Christiane Pinnekamp
Content photos unless otherwise indicated: Jessica Mienk
Editorial of the original edition: Sabine Poppe
Editorial of this edition: Stan Rawlinson
Translation: Dr Thomas Ritter
Printed by: Westermann Druck, Zwickau

All rights reserved: No part of this book may be reprinted or reproduced or utilized in any form or by any electronic, mechanical, or other means, now known or hereafter invented, including photocopying and recording, or in any information storage or retrieval system, without permission in writing from the publisher.
British Library Cataloguing in Publication Data
A catalogue record of this book is available from the British Library.

Printed in Germany

ISBN 978-0-85788-201-1

Contents

Preface

This book explores the topic of communication with dogs. When we communicate with our dog, we generally do it verbally and mostly in the form of commands: "Come!" – "Sit!" – "Down!" – "Heel!" and so on. At least that's how we learned it.

Here, on the other hand, we are talking about a predominantly non-verbal, almost intuitive, kind of communication. This requires a high degree of concentration and self discipline on the part of the human. You experience a new and different attitude towards your canine friend and towards life itself.

Our seminar participants are often very surprised how quickly you can build an exceptionally different, very close relationship with your dog. Suddenly everything seems to happen effortlessly which normally required a lot of hard work. Once the individual has changed his thinking, a type of communication is possible that is so subtle that outsiders will not even notice it.

This interspecies communication is not at all esoteric or "off the wall" – it is based on purely scientific principles, the laws of nature. It's all pure physics, as you will see in a moment. It's up to us and only us, whether we decide to go the easy, harmonious route or whether we want to continue "communicating" with our dogs by yelling loudly and yanking the lead. Start down the path of perfect harmony with your dog – take the quiet route and take your dog for what he is … *a dog!*

The "invisible lead" symbolizes the relationship with your dog.

The invisible lead

"Voluntary dependence is the most beautiful state, and how could that be possible without love?"

(Johann Wolfgang von Goethe, Die Wahlverwandtschaften)

In our book *Hundelogie – das Einsteigerbuc*h (Mienk 2008, not yet published in English) we explain in detail how to build a harmonious relationship with your dog. This harmony culminates in the "invisible lead", a close bond between dog and human that works even across long distances. The method works only if a solid bond is already in place and if you are ready to see yourself and your dog in a completely different light.

People ask us all the time how to create this intimacy. Interestingly, it is mostly the "dog training area fanatics" who look at us with indignation when they see how we communicate with our own dogs, often without any words or gestures at all. When we speak to our dogs, it is in complete, normal sen-

The lead gives your dog support, security and protects him from dangers.

The lead forms a loose connection to your dog, it doesn't tie him down.

tences: "Come on, Tony, we want to go for a walk today – or do you have other plans?" We don't need treats, force, pressure, or commands!

Our dogs don't obey – they cooperate.

If this is what we want to achieve, we first have to reverse our entire thinking and our actions. And that starts with the term "lead".

Let's redefine the term "lead":

- A lead does not hold the dog. It supports the dog.
- A lead does not secure the dog. It gives him security.
- A lead does not offer protection from the dog. It offers protection to the dog.
- A lead does not limit the dog's liberty. It gives him liberties.
- A lead does not tie the dog down – it is the (loose) connection between human and dog.

And yet it exists, after all ...

"When God measures a dog, he draws a tape around his heart instead of his head."

(Anonymous)

Who hasn't asked himself why the dog of a homeless person stays with his human in all situations without a collar or a lead while our dog is dragging us across the street at full speed on the lead. Who hasn't wondered why especially the dogs of those people who have never even seen a dog training area, always seem to do the right thing without

Dogs and humans understand each other

any commands? Who doesn't have the longing deep down inside for a "Lassie" or "Rex"? Sure, "Lassie" or "Rex" are creations of the movie industry. But the dogs of the homeless people? They are real. Our own dogs are real, too. Very real indeed. Without ever having undergone any "training", we cannot take all of them everywhere. But out of their own free will, each one of them would go through fire for us, if need be. Do you wonder why you can't do this with your dog and how to establish such a close bond? The answer is simple: We love each other, we share a life together, and we understand each other.

Four elementary things make the difference:

- The human attitude towards the dog and towards life.
- The resulting basic training.
- The bond and leadership.
- The thoughts, emotions and consequently the "invisible lead" that works extremely well for the happy ones.

Human attitudes towards dogs

"The righteous one does not need to command: and it works. Those who are not righteous may give orders: but they will not be obeyed."

(Confucius, Conversations Lunyü)

The dog is a partner – yes, but not in the human sense. Dogs always live in the here and now, fraught with all the experiences of the past. Unlike us humans, dogs do not live in the future. Thoughts like: "What's going to happen tomorrow?" are foreign to them. Neither do they think about the past: "I should have eaten the bone yesterday. Then it wouldn't have been stolen today ..."

We humans have to take dogs as they are and meet all their needs, so that they can live happily by our side as partners. Only a happy, relaxed dog is able and willing to adjust to his human in such a way that a lasting bond develops.

Contrary to popular belief, dogs do not see us as the leader of the pack. A dog knows the difference between humans and animals. He is not stupid – just different. We should therefore not act like dogs, but like humans – however, like honest humans, because good human actors are rare. And dogs see through us very quickly.

If all prerequisites are in place, I congratulate you. Then you have laid the foundation for a very harmonious co-existence. But always remember: dogs are animals, not humans – they think differently, act differently, and live differently from us humans. You can have 100 dogs of the same breed – each one

When you accept your dog as a partner the way he is, you are on the right track.

has his own unique character, each one has a different charm, and each one has a different charisma.

Dogs are unique individuals that require species specific, highly individualized interactions and communications. Communication among dogs is done mainly through gestures or through vibrations = energy.

Communication between human and dog

"It is not the goals we set for ourselves that show who we are, but the roads we take in order to reach them."

(Anonymous)

In communications between human and dog we discern:

- verbal
- nonverbal
- subconscious.

The communication scientist and psychotherapist Paul Watzlawick once said: "We cannot not communicate!" Everything we do, think, and believe is communication. Around 60 per cent of our communications are subconscious and nonverbal, 5 per cent are conscious and nonverbal, and about 35 per cent are verbal.

Our dogs respond to the slightest gestures on our part and to our vibrations. We constantly emit vibrations – good ones, bad ones, neutral ones – our dog receives them and processes them in his own way. Dogs perceive and process our nonverbal communications much more precisely than gestures or words. When we communicate with them verbally, we have to realize always that this type of communication has the lowest importance for the dog – he still relies more on our vibrations and reacts accordingly. In the process he registers – usually with special intensity – our subconscious signals: the dog reacts, but we don't realize what he reacts to.

Your dog perceives visible and invisible vibrations right away. He will respond the way you would like only when your signals are truly positive.

A practical example

Gerd lets his Newfoundland dog romp on a large field without a lead. A glance at his watch tells him that he should have been back at the office by now. He calls Blacky, he is now under time pressure. Blacky, who is usually extremely obedient, glances back briefly, but doesn't listen. Time is running out – the boss will be mad. Gerd calls again, more impatiently this time. Simultaneously, he sees the image of the furious boss in his mind, scolding him for being late. Blacky doesn't respond. Now Gerd has had enough, his anger rises. Suddenly, he remembers what he learned: "Never call your dog impatiently, always be friendly." Although he is enraged, he calls Blacky with a sugary sweet voice, and he in turn glances back briefly and increases the distance…

(Photo: Tierfotoagentur.de/K. Lührs)

What happened? Has Blacky, who is always obedient, suddenly gone crazy? Does he want to provoke his owner? Or does he simply have something better to do? No, none of the above.

Blacky could feel the vibration – "the stress" – even when he was called the first time. He becomes insecure and doesn't know what to do with this feeling of his human. So he waits. The second call tells Blacky: "His owner is annoyed." A difficult situation for Blacky: on the one hand, he wants to come back on command; on the other hand, he doesn't know why his owner is angry. No dog likes being punished for something he doesn't understand – and in this context no dog can understand anger or stress. Even the sugary sweet call doesn't fool the dog – he picks up on the negative vibrations and responds more to them than to the word.

Only when we know and accept that our dogs react more to our vibrations, our thoughts and emotions more than to anything else, we have the key to the "invisible lead".

Obedience

"One drop of love is more than an ocean of willpower and reason."

(Blaise Pascal)

A very important attitude towards our dog has to do with obedience. How do we define obedience? How important is it to us and what does it mean for a true partnership between human and dog?

In certain situations you have to be able to rely on your dog to come when you call him.

Dogs must obey – yes. In certain situations I have to be able to rely 100 per cent on my dog to obey. But it is nonsense to demand this blind obedience over and over. It is necessary that the dog comes when you call him, if a car is approaching or if there is a clear and present danger. It is nonsense for the dog to appear immediately in the house every time the human calls him, just because he wants to test his dog's "obedience" over and over again.

It is important that my dog stands or sits to wait before crossing the street. But is it really necessary for him to sit on a blanket at home, in his own territory, for hours on end without obvious reason? Why should the dog sit before he gets his food bowl? Why should he "demonstrate" sitting when his human calls him? These are all meaningless exercises that have nothing to do with communication or harmony. This does not mean that you cannot expect your dog to "demonstrate" sitting when you call him – after all, you expect your child also to "behave" at the dinner table. But you have to be aware that your dog fulfills your request without understanding the reason why. Should he omit to do it once in a while, he cannot understand why he is punished (even if it is only an impatient gesture from you).

A dog needs boundaries, where he can move freely and be himself. These boundaries should be flexible, not rigid. And a dog needs rights that nobody, not even you, is allowed to infringe up on. If I expect my dog to obey every command, every order right away, I may have an obedient dog, but no partner.

If I expect obedience from my dog, I don't need orders or commands. I need a lot of understanding, knowledge, and sensitivity for a being that is so different from us humans. This is the difference between shaping behaviour and obedience training!

A practical example

Gerda, a young woman, comes to us with her four-year-old shepherd cross Arko. She tells us desperately that she realized after reading our homepage that she had done everything wrong. Now she wants to do everything right, but Arko steadfastly refuses to cooperate even the slightest bit. She doesn't understand – until recently, Arko had passed all the tests and was very successful. Now he has suddenly started acting "crazy" at home. He doesn't obey at all any more and doesn't want to accept the new method at all.

During our conversation with Gerda, Arko sat next to her and looked at her expectantly. I asked Gerda to get up, which she did – Arko also got up right away, and went to Gerda, "heeled" like in a textbook, and looked at her expectantly. But Gerda didn't pay any attention to him. She looked at me equally expectantly. I asked both of them to sit again (which they both did as if "on command" – they were in the same position as before). I wanted to see this behaviour on her own familiar ground and made an appointment with Gerda at her home for the following day. As soon as I rang the doorbell, all hell broke loose inside. Arko barked and jumped against the door like a maniac. Then Gerda's quiet voice sounded: "No Arko, you can't do that". Gerda opened the door, and Arko jumped up at me with full force. I had seen it coming and was prepared. Then I looked at the door and said to Gerda: "You have had a lot of visitors lately, haven't you?" She nodded and explained that her landlord had complained to her and told her that she had to put in a new door.

We sat down in the living room and Gerda offered me coffee. I was not to put the cups on the table under any circumstances, however, because otherwise Arko would knock them over. So I was able to verify in person that Arko, who stayed by his owner's side out of insecurity in strange environments, acted like "Rambo" at home. So, while I explained to Gerda what she had done wrong so far, I put my cup on the

(Photo: Tierfotoagentur.de/K. Lührs)

table and watched Arko out of the corner of my eye. He immediately wanted to jump on the cup, but I stopped him through a simple: "Leave it!" which I spoke quietly, but menacingly. Arko immediately aborted his plan and looked at me puzzled. I petted him and explained to Gerda that a dog needs certain boundaries. His freedom ends where your freedom begins, and vice versa. That's the only way to live together peacefully. I explained to her in detail how to react in various situations and that she can continue to engage in dog sports with Arko. In sports, where she challenges him, commands are okay – at home she speaks in entire sentences and with emphasis.

Your dog needs independence …

but also boundaries. You have to show him where his boundaries are and where his liberty ends.

After a transition period of two weeks, both came back to me: Arko greeted me, moving around nonchalantly and self-assured. You could see how proud Gerda was of her Arko. The two of them were growing into a team now – Gerda set the boundaries that both respected. Of course that was only the very first step towards perfect harmony – but every journey begins with the first step ...

Another example

Gunther is a thirty-something first dog owner with a female shepherd dog. He loves dogs and especially his Little One. He bought Little One from a breeder at 14 weeks, but left her with friends so that she could grow up in a pack. It was only months later that he brought her home. But although both love each other very much, Gunther has problems with Little One, who is now a little over a year old and no longer plays with other dogs. She is lazy and sleeps most of the day. She doesn't like to go for walks any more, doesn't like to fetch sticks, doesn't go into the water and is afraid of all sorts of things. Little One is a very beautiful Old German shepherd dog. Gunther thinks that having a bond should be sufficient – after all he loves her, the right bond is there – so what is wrong with the dog? Gunther is at his wit's end. He does everything for his dog: he shares his food with her, his bed, his couch, his hobbies ... she has to do nothing that she doesn't like. If she doesn't want to go out – then they don't go outside. If she wants to go in the car instead of going for a walk, she can go in the car. She goes without a lead most of the time – when she met other dogs in the past, she used to run towards them right away and wanted to play.

(Photo: Tierfotoagentur.de/D. Geithner)

In this case the solution is very simple as well: love alone is not enough! A dog needs guidelines, just like a young human. Shaping the behaviour of Little One had been completely overlooked. Gunther was her friend, but not her "leader". A dog needs as much loving guidance as a well organized team. And "leadership" is always required – every day, every hour, every minute, every second. Leadership means giving guidance, protection and instruction, but at the same time also a level of freedom. In addition, as an Old German shepherd dog, she needs more boundaries than some other dogs. She needs a job, an occupation – fetching a stick or playing ball is not her thing. Gunther didn't understand that dogs play differently from humans – and now he is disappointed. We show Gunther and Little One what is possible, including thinking exercises and slow games. We explain to Gunther that shaping behaviour is necessary, and that it takes a lot of time. A shepherd dog that is kept in accordance with the needs of his species has specific qualities that need to be supported in order for him to be happy and content. And now, since Gunther has become not just a friend, but also a friendly "leader", both are happy and content. Even the dog's fear issues suddenly disappeared.

A dog needs rules – which he learns through shaping behaviour, not through submission or drill. A dog needs security – which only a human can give him.

The obedience that is necessary in order to achieve cooperation and communication differs from one individual to another – it depends on the life circumstances, the place of residence and many other components.

Our own dogs learn the following rules from day one:

- Stealing is not allowed! They may not steal from the table, or from any other areas.
- My food belongs to me – your food belongs to you.
- You stop or sit before crossing the street.
- You don't jump up on strangers.
- When we are outside together (outside the property), the dog has to come right away when called.

There are more rules that may vary from case to case – and from dog to dog.

You see, we don't care whether the dog sits or lies down on command or request – the basic rules must be obeyed. Within these rules, our dogs can move around. What is especially important is that we must also adhere to the rules and boundaries as well.

These are the rules for the humans:

- The dog is not to be disturbed when he is eating.
- When the dog is asleep we leave him alone if possible.
- The dog is allowed to retreat when children or visitors are too much for him.

Your dog has the right to escape to a safe place without being bothered.

- When children are visiting or in the house, they must learn to treat the dog "reasonably".
- The dog is protected by me – if need be, even from my own family.

These rules have nothing to do with the particular training of the dogs. I have dogs that passed all monitoring tests with excellencye – they look at it like we do: the dog training area is sport. At home we still speak in complete sentences with a lot of gesturing and also nonverbal communication.

So you only have rules and don't expect absolute total obedience from your dog? Then we come to the next issue – the basic training.

Basic training

"Patience is the time it takes to understand everything."

(Anonymous)

By basic training, we mean the foundation, the basic rules that every dog must follow and obey:

- being housebroken (unless a physical or psychological cause prevents it)
- knowing his name and responding to it
- "mastering" everyday life situations with his human.

Exercises like "sit", "down", etc. are not a part of this stage, which does not mean that

Your dog has to learn to "master" everyday life situations together with you.

they are not useful, however. The everyday life situations vary, depending on where you live, (city or countryside), environment (deer, joggers, bikers) and the individual living environment.

You see there are very few things your dog really has to do. You make the rules. You are the master of all resources. You are responsible for your dog. You are the older, more experienced one, and you pass your knowledge and your experience on to your dog – you are the teacher.

Show your dog the dangers of everyday life: traffic, strange humans, strange dogs, and teach him to follow certain rules for his own safety:

- Don't jump in front of cars; instead, stand or sit by the side of the road.
- Don't chase joggers; instead, stay close to your human.
- Don't approach every strange dog; instead, wait for your human to judge the situation.

Show your dog that he can trust you implicitly – that you protect him from all the perils of daily life and that you help him to get along in human society.

Knowing and getting to know each other

Bonding also means "knowing". Our dogs get to know us very well given time – often even better than we know ourselves. They can tell the difference when we are serious or not, when we are willing to compromise or when we will not accept certain behaviours.

Earlier in this book I said: "My food is mine". It's up to me whether I share it with

my dogs. From time to time, my dogs also get something – yes, even at the table. And at the next meal they stand right there, asking if they can have something to eat. A slight head-shaking on my part is enough to send them on their way and go about their business – they don't beg! So they learn over time when "No" really means "No" and when it means "Maybe" – and they act accordingly. It is helpful if you are aware of whether you are willing to compromise or not. You will also get to know your dog better on a daily basis, if you make the effort.

Observe your dog and his reactions very closely – the better you know each other, the easier it is to develop a bond to the point where it becomes a connection.

The rhythm of life

"Where would you recover from the endless deceit, falseness and backstabbing of humankind if it were not for the dogs into whose honest face you can look without distrust?"

(Arthur Schopenhauer)

Although dogs are true masters of adaptation, they have a completely different rhythm of life from humans. Dogs usually don't sleep through the night – they take naps throughout the day. Dogs need much more exercise than humans, and different kinds of exercise. Dogs have different times of digestion than humans – a fact that we have to take into consideration for exercise. Dogs – typically – don't like being alone. But many dogs have to stay by themselves during the day, because their humans have to earn their feed. These dogs are then full of energy when we come home tired. This excess energy ("That was so boring, Mum, now do something, do something, play with me …!") is discharged the moment we open the front door. The dog is happy and leaps up and down on us, full of anticipation – and that makes us annoyed. How often is the dog scolded and punished

Full of longing and boredom, your dog waits for you to come home.

for his excess energy, his expectation of us? That's not exactly a basis for trust, but this is precisely the foundation for the "invisible lead", for bonding, for a relationship – this is important to understand!

The world from your dog's perspective

"The more I have learned, the more I have learned that learning never stops."

(Anonymous)

Your dog sees the world differently, very differently from you. That is, on the one hand, due to the way he is built – he walks on four legs. On the other hand, it is due to his size – he is, even if he is a very large dog, only three feet tall (at the withers). The third factor is that he is equipped with completely different abilities, especially as far as his perception is concerned (instinct, motor skills, smell, eyes, ears, tactile sense).

We want to talk about the "world view" of our four-legged friends. In order to understand the "world view" of our quadrupeds even remotely, we like to perform the following experiment in our workshops and seminars, which you should try at home.

You need at least two adults and, ideally, one child. You go down on all fours and wander from room to room, while the people around you go about their daily routine: cleaning, straightening up, talking, receiving visitors, and so on. They have to treat you like a dog: you have to move out of the way when they come, move to the side, you may not go into certain rooms, and you are sent to your place (a blanket on the floor), as soon as you are in the way, somehow.

Remember that you may not use your hands like a human. You can hardly defend yourself against the annoying child that might be fussing around you constantly. You have to be on your guard all the time so that nobody steps on your "paws" or on your "tail". If you can last for 30 minutes like this, you will have had enough and you will feel, frankly, pretty superfluous and tiny. Remember this feeling every time you interact with your dog!

Everything around you is huge – now imagine the whole thing outside – not a pleasant feeling, is it? What makes it even tougher for the dog, is that he is not allowed to vocalize most of the time – he is certainly not allowed to bark excessively (if at all). If he whines, his human is either startled or he scolds the dog. If he gets up from his spot, because he is bored, the human gets annoyed, because the dog is in the way again. Can you put yourself in your dog's place? Can you sense his emotions? If so, you are on the right path – then it is not far to the "invisible lead".

Go down on all fours and experience the world from the perspective of your dog.

The connection

"Sometimes you think that strength consists in holding on. But it is letting go that shows true strength."

(Anonymous)

The closer the bond between you and your dog, the more your friend reflects your emotions, your moods, and your character. It is true that the dog is the mirror of your soul. That is why you have to take responsibility from the very first moment and be a role model for your dog. You have to give him support, protect him, help him; in short, be a loving "leader". A good leader is a mixture of:

- thirty per cent understanding "mother/father"
- thirty per cent loving teacher
- twenty per cent friend who forgives everything
- ten per cent coach with psychological training
- twenty per cent robust playmate.

Did you do the maths? Correct – a good "leader" always gives 110 per cent!

It's not difficult *becoming* a leader – but much harder staying one.

"A human who needs to have patience as an educator is a poor devil. What he needs is love and joy!"

(Johann Heinrich Pestalozzi)

It is interesting to note in this context how the term alpha-male or alpha-female is misused in various idiomatic phrases. In its original meaning, alpha referred not to the strong, dominant ruler over his "people", but to a person who was in an alpha state at all times. Alpha state means being psychologically balanced, being able to cope with any situation, assuming responsibility for others, never getting into the beta state which equals panic. In other words, alpha is a reliable, self-assured "leader".

You become the "leader" the moment you see your dog for the first time, whether it is the cute puppy at the breeder's or your great love from the shelter. With this first look you create the bond that will bind the two of you together in the future. When you bring your dog home, you straightaway have to become the leader – you can't practise, you have to be it. This is extremely difficult for many people, because human nature, human idiosyncrasies, the entire palette of human "vibrations", immediately assault the dog and begin to shape the relationship.

Mutual love and trust – the dog trusts his human and vice versa.

A practical example

Eva came to us, desperate like many of our "clients". Her year-old female Malinois was timid and didn't come when she was called. Instead, she ran away ... The first contact between Eva and me was on the phone. She sounded nervous, but tried to describe the situation with humour. When we met in person, my perception turned out to be accurate: Eva is a shy, slightly insecure person. Her dog was the exact mirror image of Eva – nervous, insecure, anxiety ridden. At the slightest incident, both of them fed off each other's emotions.

During a walk, I noticed that both of them were extremely aware of every rustling of the leaves, every little sound. Both were pure tension. When I asked Eva to let the dog off the lead in a large meadow, she answered: "She won't come when I call!" It was only when I lied to Eva, saying that there was a fence behind the embankment so that the dog wouldn't be able to run away, that she released the (visible as well as the invisible) lead and the dog ran a few yards ahead. After a few minutes I asked Eva to call the dog. Knowing that her darling could not be very far away, Eva called Fibi in a relaxed manner and the dog returned right away. (More about Eva's history in the next chapter.)

You can't deceive a dog. It is useless if you merely act confidently. It does not work if you pretend to be a strong character – the dog knows the truth from the first second.

(Photo: Tierfotoagentur.de/M. Häupl)

But a good "leader" also trusts his dog, who can gauge certain situations much better than we humans. An unbiased dog can judge much better than ourselves whether a stranger poses a danger or not. A dog also senses much sooner whether there is a hidden danger in the forest (such as an old, almost filled-in well, perhaps).

Mutual respect – mutual love and mutual trust are the prerequisites for the "invisible lead". In order for everything to work, you have to learn to control your words, your gestures, your emotions, and your thoughts at all times.

Dog whispering – literally!

I am often astonished at how loud and aggressive many people are in the dog training area. They yell at the top of their lungs, they command, they threaten, they curse, and they complain about their dog. Rarely, very rarely have I seen "dog training area people" smile or laugh during the work. If you consider that dogs can hear a hundred times better than us the noise must be deafening for the poor animals on a constant basis. This is bad for the ears, the mind, and the soul. The drill sergeant's tone has disappeared from many barracks of the world – but in our dog training areas this tone still lingers on. Why should we change something that has been like this for many years? We would have to change our thinking. That would be asking too much, or would it?

You want to improve, otherwise you would not be reading this book. Then start right away: whisper from now on. I mean that literally – this has nothing to do with the so-called "dog whisperers". Speak softly with your dog – he will listen to you far better.

A practical example
I am constantly surrounded by at least twelve dogs of all age groups. When they play and romp we have the noise level of a disco. I sometimes try to shout over the noise. That works – for exactly ten seconds – then it starts up again. When I say very quietly: shhhhh ... it is suddenly quiet – you can hear a pin drop – every dog comes to me. Then I can tell them quietly to go easy on my ears. That has always worked so far.

Why should we desensitize our dogs through a loud drill sergeant tone? Nobody has really been able to explain that to me yet. You are probably going to use the distance argument: if my dog is 100 yards away, I have to yell. Either that or I have a little whistle – a very brief burst is enough – the dog looks at me and I can indicate to him through my gestures that I want him to come to me. This method has proven to be more pleasant for the dog, the human, and the environment.

Thought connection

"Watch your thoughts – for they turn into words. Watch your words – for they turn into actions."

(Talmud)

You probably know the proverb. We will add: "Watch your emotions – for they turn into thoughts."

In order for the "invisible lead" to work you have to focus on your thoughts.

Back to Eva: Eva's example demonstrates very nicely how the "invisible lead" works. Fibi did not come when she was being called, as long as Eva was convinced that her dog would ignore the call. Eva's fear that the dog could escape was too great. Only when I convinced Eva that Fibi couldn't go beyond the embankment, Eva believed it and was convinced that it was impossible to run away. With this conviction, she called Fibi, who came right away.

What happened? If you want to achieve the desired results, mutual attentiveness = concentration is essential. At some point before our meeting, Eva's concentration had wavered in a moment of inattentiveness, or she was paying attention to something else when she called Fibi. The dog sensed the moment of inattentiveness and did not respond to the call. On the contrary, she moved farther away from Eva. Ever since that time, Eva was convinced that Fibi wouldn't listen.

She passed this thought on to Fibi every time she called her. Why should the dog listen, when she encountered such negative vibrations? On our walk together, I suggested to Eva that there was no way Fibi could run away (Eva's big fear). I got Eva to call Fibi and convinced her at the same time that Fibi would respond immediately to the call no matter what. I was able to clear out any negative thought in Eva for a few seconds. At the same time, I asked Eva what the most beautiful experience with Fibi had been, so that for a very short time she emitted only positive vibrations (thoughts and emotions).

Another practical example

Askan, a Jack Russell Terrier, is vivacious and a typical terrier with a huge amount of self confidence. His "leader" loves him more than anything, but she was afraid to let him off the lead. "Askan will go hunting, he follows every scent" Sonja claimed. She didn't even have any bad experiences. She was simply told as a first time dog owner that all terriers are hunters.

I took a walk with her on our property, but I brought along one of our female dogs, Candy. I convinced Sonja that Askan would definitely stay with Candy at all times and

(Photo: Tierfoto-agentur.de/Alexa P.)

proved that Candy would come immediately when I called her.*Askan was on a lead the whole time. Candy was free. When I felt that Sonja believed me, I let her take the lead off Askan. He was happy about his freedom and raced around in the wood (it was our own wood, no hunters, no dangers!).

After a few minutes of intense conversation with Sonja I asked her to call Askan in a friendly and joyful way. She knelt down and recalled her dog. He came running right away, and Sonja was as happy as a child, which she showed Askan clearly. Candy was nowhere to be seen. She only showed up when I called her. So Askan had come to his owner out of his own free will. Both had an extremely positive experience that way: Sonja trusted that Askan always listened and Askan obeyed because Sonja was so happy about it. We repeated the "game" two more times on that same day, and twice the following week on a different piece of property. Both had deeply internalized the positive thoughts.

** Here you find a contradiction: on the one hand, I claim that I will never call a dog without reason, that I never call a dog just to prove his prompt obedience – and now this: I call Candy multiple times only to prove that she always obeys! Very simple: we have several dogs that we use as "therapy dogs" – Candy is one of them. For these dogs it is a "job" to help other dogs and their people – they like doing their job and they are "rewarded" accordingly.*

Since then, Askan listens to every call of his owner's right away, regardless of what he is busy doing. But Sonja never calls Askan without a reason. She always gives him a reason to listen – be it that the walk continues, that she starts a game with him, or that both simply go home.

How is all of this possible and how can thoughts influence events so much over long distances? Is it magic, voodoo? Is it spiritual? Weirdness? Not at all. It is all simply a law of nature, which we like to deny.

Has it never happened to you before that you thought of someone and suddenly that person calls you on the phone? Do you know the feeling that something is going to happen – and then it does? Have you ever sat at a table in a restaurant and felt that somebody was watching you – without you seeing it? Have the hairs on the back of your neck stood on end when you saw a total stranger? This is exactly what nonverbal communication is about. This often works across long distances.

We have done the following experiment with our future trainers. Four student trainers were sitting on a large meadow with their dogs. The dogs were close to their owners, but not on a lead. The student trainers had to prevent their dogs from running towards a familiar person who was calling the dog only by thinking very firmly: "No!" We conducted this experiment individually and the result was devastating for some of the participants:

Dog A – Owner A

Dog A jumps up as soon as the friend calls him. Owner A is sitting on a chair, all her muscles taut to breaking point. She is concentrating. Dog A takes two hesitant steps forward – the owner's muscles tighten even more – her face is grimacing from the effort. She is not allowed to move, only to think: "No!" When her concentration slackens after three minutes – the dog rushes off. For three minutes she kept her dog only through her thoughts. Then she let go of the "invisible lead.

Dog B – Owner B

The friend comes and calls. Dog B is sitting in front of owner B, pure tension – he is sitting. Owner B is concentrating, but not nearly as much as Owner A – she closes her eyes. Only after ten minutes and many desperate calls by the friend does she releases the "invisible lead", exhales – and Dog B races off.

What was the difference? Owner A was not as advanced yet at this point. Her dog hesitated because she was working so terribly hard, but he didn't leave. Owner B already knew about this phenomenon, without having really tried it. But she approached the issue in a much more relaxed manner. Later she told me that she closed her eyes, tuned out her ears and visualized the image of her dog sitting in front of her. Owner A only kept thinking "No!", "No!", "No!" as hard as she could.

The two other participants did not succeed at all. During a later meeting and a similar exercise they were able to succeed as well. They had realized during the first attempt that their bond with their dogs was not strong enough.

Once again this has nothing to do with voodoo – it is not even real telepathy. The stronger your bond becomes with your dog, the more he will respond to your vibrations – voluntarily, because with your thoughts you can hardly hold him against his will.

The real magic word, the key to everything we want to achieve is: free will.
A living being that does something voluntarily will do it happily and with full energy. A living being that is forced to do something may do it, too, but only under protest.

If you go outside with your dog now, take the lead off and think he will come to you

before he gets run over by a bus just because you call him in your thoughts, think again. Say good-bye to your dog. Every road – no matter how long – begins with the first step. Practice, practice, practice!

More simply put: your thoughts and emotions determine your reality and that of your dog.

Natural law

"It is absolutely possible that there are untold worlds hidden beyond the perception of our senses."

(Albert Einstein)

This thought connection is no weirdness, there is nothing esoteric about it, and it has nothing to do with the kind of "animal communication" that you are familiar with from the media. It is simply a law of nature which we can follow or ignore. This law says that everything in the universe consists of energy. Every piece of furniture, every tree, everything basically consists of energy. If you take a chair apart into its smallest components, what remains beyond the atom is energy. Our brain emits energy, too – all the time. Brain waves can be measured, they are real. Every thought, conscious or subconscious, is pure energy. Energy is released and can therefore be transmitted. This applies to positive as well as negative energy. It's pure physics, a law of nature, when we utilize this energy to achieve a solid basis in interspecies communication – a kind of communication that could not be more difficult.

The dog as a mirror of the human soul

"When a human soul meets a dog soul in paradise, the human soul has to bow to the dog's soul."

(Siberian proverb)

It is often said that the dog is the mirror of our soul. I used this term in the chapter on "Bonding" as well. Now we want to take a closer look at it. Remember that your

Always remember: you alone are responsible for your dog's behaviour.

thoughts and emotions create your world and that of your dog. Be careful – it could be that you don't like what comes next:

- If you have a dog who is nervous, fearful, aggressive, or whatever, then only one person is responsible for it: you!
- If you have a dog who doesn't come when you call him, only one person is responsible: you!
- If you cannot depend on your dog, if he runs away, barks at strangers or attacks them, or if he runs away from strangers, or is "stubborn", only one person is responsible: you!
- If your dog is annoying, hyperactive and out of control in some daily routine situations, only one person is responsible: you!

Remember Eva's story. Eva was a kind, but very insecure person, who was afraid of all kinds of things. She was extremely tense in her interactions with others, but also by herself. And what was her dog, Fibi, like? The exact mirror image. The story only changed when I suggested to Eva that nothing could happen, that she could trust me completely. After the first success, Eva's self confidence and with that Fibi's self confidence grew as well.

This book is full of examples like this – you only have to look behind the facade. We cannot separate human psychology and animal psychology. That's exactly why so many dog training or consultation sessions with dog therapists fail or show no results. First the human has to learn, then the dog will be no problem.

An example from my own life

I, too, have times when I'm in a bad mood and forget everything I know about educating dogs, times in which really everything goes wrong, until I manage to sort out my thoughts and emotions and to channel them into the right direction. That's what happened with our Jack Russell Terrier Tony, a typical member of his breed – always upbeat, always in the mood for pranks, self confident like a large animal – just a great Jack. Unfortunately, also a terrier who likes to seek and find and who hates boredom.

We were on a walk – I was in a terrible mood, as I had mentioned, and had "instigated" this walk with my daughter Tony and Cisquo to relax. The dogs were running off the lead across a large meadow. On the other side of the meadow was a path, then another meadow and then ... the road. Silent and lost in thought, we were both walking along. Suddenly, Tony ran like crazy farther and farther away from us. My daughter called Cis and I yelled for Tony – Cis came but Tony ran as fast as his little legs would carry him in the opposite direction. I got mad and yelled like a maniac: "Tony!!!!" I also started to become afraid that he might run across the street – pure panic mixed with anger.

My daughter advised me calmly to organize my thoughts and emotions and to call Tony calmly. But I was still so caught up in my anger that nothing worked any more. My daughter called Tony – he came a little closer. By now I was convinced that the "stupid dog won't listen to me anyway today". Tony came within a few yards and then raced off in the opposite direction. My daughter made a bratty remark and I exploded, yelled at her and provoked a fight – thank God! Seconds later I had regained my composure. I was able to organize my thoughts and emotions and send positive thoughts and emotions to Tony. I called Tony quietly – much too quietly for the large distance. He turned towards me and came running as fast as his little legs would carry him. He jumped into my arms, wagged his tail, and licked me. Tears welled up in my eyes. Later I stood in front of the mirror, the real one of glass, looking at myself: "You stupid cow!"

(Photo: Tierfotoagentur.de/S. Schwerdtfeger)

Another example

Corinna owned the shepherd-collie-mix Rocky. She bought the dog after her first dog had passed away. Corinna and her partner Regine were living in a big city. There were problems with the puppy right from the beginning. The other dogs bit him, there was no obedience, he became housebroken very late, and he hurt himself all the time, was sick and saw the vet more often than the others. They were very careful with him: they only fed him venison meat and cooked rice because his digestive system rebelled. He went mostly on a lead, because otherwise he would run away and hurt himself.

When Rocky turned two, he gradually became really "weird". He wouldn't allow them to dry him off after being bathed, acting afraid at first, then aggressively. Then he wouldn't be brushed any more – again acting fearful at first, then aggressively. He was also afraid of the chest harness being put on. The owners drove from dog trainer to dog trainer, from animal psychologist to animal psychologist. Nothing worked. Sooner or later the situation escalated with a trainer to the point that Rocky bit the coat collar of one of his owners in mid leap.

Meanwhile, Rocky also acted highly aggressive around other dogs as well. That's how the three of them arrived here. Corinna, tall and acting very self confidently, Regine, small, very nervous and anxious, and Rocky, a total mixture of both women. For one week we tried everything to "change" the two humans. But they were so entangled in their many issues that we were unable to extricate them. They felt very limited by Rocky in some ways (because Rocky could not stay alone) and kept comparing poor Rocky with their previous dog who never made any mistakes, in their memory, of course.

In addition to all the issues of his humans, Rocky also felt that he was unable to satisfy their demands. The three of them had wanted to stay for three weeks – but after one week, I sent the owners back into their city and kept Rocky with us. I tried to convince them that their thinking and feeling needed to be "remodelled". In the meantime, Rocky was assigned a kennel between a female and a male, was fed regular dog food and, like all of our own dogs, fresh, raw meat on a regular basis.

This went on for several weeks. Rocky had become used to the other dogs over time, he even played with the female sometimes. His physical health was excellent as well. But every evening his owners called and Rocky showed extreme reactions to these phone calls, whether he was present or not: sometimes he became aggressive, sometimes depressed. One day when I was on the phone with his owners, Rocky was taking a walk in the woods with our groomer. She told me later that at one point he suddenly stopped playing from one second to the next and trotted reluctantly beside her. You see how thoughts and emotions are effective over very large distances.

It could not go on like this. I decided to end the phone calls. The inevitable happened: Several weeks later the owners were supposed to pick up their retrained dog. Rocky had been a normal dog for all these weeks, came right away when we called him, played with other dogs, we could bathe him, dry him, brush him. I sent all three for a walk by themselves. Ten minutes later Rocky came back – alone. I saw Corinna and Regine on a large meadow, about one kilometre away. He had snapped at Regine again. Now his fate was sealed: he had to leave his owners. Long conversations ensued. Rocky stayed with us at first until he found a new home with different people.

What had happened? Corinna and Regine loved their dog, but had themselves many issues, self doubts, and fear. Both saw the entire world only in a negative light: the other bad dogs had done something to Rocky, the trainers were all incompetent (not true at all), the world was so bad, mean and nasty to them. In their anxiety they had wrapped Rocky "in cotton wool" so that he couldn't be a dog any more. All the negative feelings and thoughts had transferred themselves to the dog and manifested in him as in the owners. It was impossible to help all three.

The two ladies didn't buy another dog. They arrived at the conclusion that life with a dog was not the right thing for them. This is one of the very few cases in which we advised a separation – for everybody's benefit.

But don't worry: if you are ready to change your thinking and feeling, if you are willing to be helped and if you want to have the perfect, phenomenal relationship with your dog, you can do it. You only have to want it and do it! This book can help you, and there are still our courses, seminars, and workshops.

That's how easy it is

"Frequently, the prophecy is the main cause for the prophesied event."

(Thomas Hobbes)

Most of us have heard of the "self-fulfilling prophecy". This means that if I'm convinced that something won't work, then it isn't going to work. And vice versa, of course. If I assume, right off the bat, that my dog won't respond to being called, this negative energy = vibrations is transmitted to the dog. He feels something negative and responds with insecurity. The consequence is that he hesitates – but the human thinks: "he is disobedient". The negative vibrations increase. The dog sees no reason now to heed the call, as he "senses" something bad.

It works the other way around, too. I assume that my dog is obedient, my call sounds more positive, the energy I am sending out and the vibrations the dog is receiving are positive. He looks forward to his human and obeys immediately. Now it is important for us to react properly. When my dog comes after I have called him, I squat down and go crazy with joy. My facial expressions, my gestures, my thoughts, and my words are pure joy (yes, I often look ridiculous in public because of it – so what – my dog is worth it to me). The dog has to feel that I am overjoyed when he comes. Every second of his life he has to feel first and foremost that I love him – unconditionally.

When I'm in a bad mood or have to reprimand him (yes, that happens too, of course), he doesn't carry a grudge – my love still stands above everything else. He knows I love him, no matter what happens. Love is ever present and takes precedence. That only works if the bond between dog and human is close, very close.

When a child "screws up", I reprimand him too – yet he knows that no matter what happens, nothing changes my love for him. As soon as the punishment is over, everything is forgotten.

And there we have it – the crux of the matter – why many human–dog relationships don't really work. The main ingredient is missing: love. Many people have a problem with the term "love". That's why here is the definition from the online dictionary "Wikipedia", which I like very much: "… based on this primary meaning, the term has always been used in the colloquial language and in tradition in a symbolic sense as well, and generally refers to the strongest form of affinity feeling for other living beings, things, activities or ideas. So, this general interpretation understands love as an expression of deep appreciation. But love is also the strongest flow of energy ..."

This is the least we should offer our animals. It is more difficult to love a living being unconditionally, because we all have conditions and expectations tied to our actions: I love you, so you have to love me too! Those who manage to offer a living being this expression of deep appreciation without having any expectations in return don't need to worry about their relationships (I'm not talking just about dogs here).

A question that I often ask of my clients and seminar participants concerns love: "Do you love your dog?" Or: "How do you feel about your dog?" Some time ago I got the answer: "I like my dog very much, I'm almost in love with him." This sentence was followed by a discussion whether animals are worth less than humans. My question why that should be so still hasn't been answered.

The self-fulfilling prophecy – you believe that your dog will come when you call him, he obeys, and you go crazy with joy.

Do you love your dog without having any expectations? Then you are on the way to a close bond.

The fact is: Someone who does not give his dog the love he deserves, will never be able to form the kind of bond that is close enough for the "invisible lead". Someone who considers an animal as worth less than a human makes it "replaceable". The animal feels this very acutely and consequently makes the human "replace-able" as well. At best you get a student–teacher relationship, a temporary relationship ...

We could philosophize about this now, because in my opinion this is precisely what makes human relationships fail so often, too. The partner is exchangeable – every relationship is temporary ... Just think about it.

Stumbling blocks along the way – human inadequacy

*"If you want something you have never had,
then do something you have never done."*

(Nossrat Peseschkian)

Unfortunately, we don't live exclusively in the here and now – we have worries, we have to go to work, take the car to the shop, cook, clean, and many other things. Yesterday weighs on us, and tomorrow weighs on many of us even more. We are full of issues and are relatively rarely in a good mood. We don't exactly perceive our environment as positive, and there is little that really fills us with optimism. We are often moody and not very easy to understand for our dogs.

I have a few dogs here who make a wide berth around me when they feel that I'm in a bad mood – others make a point of coming to me and trying to make me feel better. Usually both are helpful: I feel guilty

Human inadequacy – your dog doesn't understand why he has to "function" in the dog-training area.

towards those who avoid me, and I can't be angry when I look into the faithful eyes of those who want to make me feel better. So, we have made it a habit to hit the punch bag when we are in a bad mood, or to make faces in front of the mirror, or even to complete a workout routine. Those who know me know how hard that is for me. But it helps. Because if there is anybody who doesn't deserve our foul mood, it's our dog (animal).

Animals have a hard time coping when they don't understand us and our reactions.

This is also the reason why the pure "dog training area" training doesn't work: The dog doesn't understand at all why he has to repeat each exercise ad nauseam – he doesn't understand why he has to throw himself to the ground as if he were attacked by a dragon, over and over when we call (mostly it's rather a scream) "Lie down!" He cannot understand why he has to sit over and over on a fenced property, while we walk a few steps away, only to call him to us again. To the dog, this is at best human inadequacy – some dogs tolerate this patiently their whole life, but many go on strike sooner or later – and that's what brings the so-called "problem dogs" to us – the ones with "behavioural disorders". If we are honest, we have to admit that we are the ones with the behavioural disorders – we are the "problem humans". The "invisible lead" doesn't work if we don't get our inadequacy under control. I can speak from my own painful experience here. It should be a warning and an incentive for you to check yourself, your thoughts and emotions all the time.

A practical example

One day one of our clients brought a friend with her. This friend – Babsi – had brought a little Tibetan Terrier called Bobby home from the breeder as her first dog. Babsi had been "through" all the dog schools and trainers within a radius of several hundred kilometres – her "problem" with Bobby got worse and worse: he didn't come when she called him and if he finally decided to come several long minutes later, he always stopped a few yards away from her and raced off as soon as she tried to "catch" him. That was terrible because Babsi wanted so much to have a dog to accompany her in her many athletic activities (jogging, mountain climbing, swimming in the ocean). If the dog can never go off the leash it's no fun for either one.

One day really nothing worked any more – the relationship consisted only of distrust, fear and caution. In this situation Babsi, Bobby, the petite little daughter (5) and the son (7) arrived at our house. I want to repeat the brief conversation between Babsi and myself here:

I: "What's the trouble?"

Babsi: "The dog doesn't come when I call him."

I: "Is that all?"

Babsi: "No, the dog growls at me."

I: "Really?"

Babsi: "I'm afraid that he may bite the kids."

I: "The dog?"

Babsi: "Yes, he gets really nasty."

I: "Tell me more."

(Photo: Tierfotoagentur.de/M. Häupl)

☞

Babsi: "The dog has been with us for a year now – we got him from the breeder. They told us this breed would be the best for us. The dog supposedly loved children, was easy to train and very athletic. Initially, everything was good, but then he wouldn't come any more when I called him. So I started catching him every time. It got worse and worse. A hunter told me to put a choke collar on him with a long leash and to yank so hard that he flips over on his back when he doesn't come as soon as I call him."

I: "Stop – did you do that?"

Babsi, bright red in the face: "Twice. Then I felt sorry for him. He was only four months old."

I (trying to stay calm): "Okay – continue."

Babsi: "It's got worse and worse since then. I went to a number of trainers. Now he only comes within two metres of me, if at all – even in the house. For the last few weeks he has been growling at me when I want to take something away from him."

I: "How is Bobby with the children?"

Babsi: "He hasn't done anything to them yet, but that will probably change, too."

Now I had finally heard enough. Did you notice something in the conversation? No? Babsi never once called her dog by his name. And everything was very reproachful: "The dog did …"

So we first went to our fenced area. Babsi was supposed to let her Bobby off the lead there.

She did so and glanced at me with pure despair. I promised her to catch Bobby – even it if took until night-time (it was ten o'clock in the morning). Bobby moved away very slowly, but went farther and farther. He wasn't running, he was walking. Farther and farther. He snooped his way to the fence opposite us – several hundred yards away from us.

Now Babsi had to call him. She did: "Bobby – Heeeere!" Bobby looked back – and stayed where he was. It took almost half an hour until Bobby came within two metres of Babsi. Babsi wanted to "catch" him and threw herself at him. I had seen enough, sent Babsi out of the area and asked the little daughter to call the dog. She cooed with her little voice: "Bobby – come to me?" You cannot imagine what happened then: Bobby looked around to see where she was and raced like a maniac towards the little girl. She laughed and petted her Bobby.

Babsi had been watching from a distance. I saw a tear running down her cheek. Babsi understood quickly. Three long conversations ensued – only between myself and Babsi, while the children played outside with the dogs (including Bobby) under the supervision of my daughter. Babsi needed a thorough "brain and heart washing". But she realized quickly that it wasn't "the dog" – it was Babsi herself who needed it.

It only took Babsi six weeks to change her thinking, to allow and amplify feelings – four months later Bobby always went along: to go climbing, jogging, swimming – he always ran along without a lead. He often even waited somewhere without a lead until his owner came back. There was no more fear – meanwhile there is a second dog in the family who is also allowed to go everywhere with the family just like Bobby. But why did the problem arise in the first place?

Similar to Eva, there was a situation sometime in the beginning when Babsi was distracted and Bobby didn't come when she called him. She called him again, but this time with the energetic vibration of impatience. You know the rest. The situation escalated – the more negative the vibrations were that Babsi sent out, the worse Bobby felt – he reacted in his own way. After the so-called "training" with the hunter, Bobby also became afraid of pain. Of course he didn't want to expose himself to this and so he didn't even go near Babsi any more. She in turn became angrier and more insecure ...

That's how it can go. If you don't interrupt the vicious cycle abruptly and change your thinking, critically examining yourself and your actions and reactions with a "magnifying glass", you will form a "problem dog".

The whining and blaming behaviour

I get e-mails and phone calls on a daily basis from truly desperate people that all begin with: "The dog is afraid ...; the dog is dominant ...; the dog doesn't listen ..." and other words that are constantly repeated.

I thought for a long time about whether I should confront people with the truth. Now I will simply do it through this book (that way I will be out of their immediate reach). We humans who love our dogs so much are always so lightning fast with our judgment. Instead of asking ourselves what we do wrong in our interactions with the dog, we lay the responsibility and the blame on the dog and bury ourselves in a whiny attitude that is unparalleled: "I would, but the dog ..." Is that not a great excuse for our own inadequacy? Now you are probably shocked – that's good. And so that you know what I mean I will tell you a true story.

A practical example

From time to time we take in dogs from friends to raise them in order to socialize them well and to get them used to other dogs. Mimei was one of them. She came with her half sister Shinya (my female shepherd dog) and was supposed to stay with us for half a year. Normally, I never have a problem building a relationship with a dog quickly. But when a dog is here with us only for a limited time I have to keep my feelings in check. That means I create a "half bond" with that particular dog so that we don't get too attached to each other.

Mimei was only 12 weeks old when she came. I don't know why, but I had problems with Mimei right from the beginning – she was so very different from our own dogs – I can't even explain the difference precisely. I liked her, but I couldn't develop a real bond with her. Certain circumstances led to Mimei staying with us. Now I had a real problem: because of my occasional distant attitude towards Mimei she did not exactly open up to me either. She went to my husband to be scratched. When she had done something naughty, she hid. And she was naughty a lot: she stole from the kitchen, urinated everywhere she went, barked like crazy without any discernible reason, chewed up furniture and had a craving for plastic bottles, which she found everywhere and destroyed passionately. I was aggravated beyond belief and scolded her all the time. That didn't help our relationship, of course. I actually fell into the whining and blaming behaviour: "Mimei is crazy, she is completely nuts, Mimei is stupid ...".

The harder I tried to get a connection with her, the crazier Mimei became. Whenever I saw her, she had done something naughty. To make things worse, she became sick and I had to give her injections and medication every day, which hurt our relationship more than it helped. Because I never talked about the things that bothered me nobody could pull me out of this whining behaviour. They only wondered about the strange behaviour we were displaying towards each other. Mimei was the first dog in a long time from whom I demanded to sit and lie down as the first thing (she still doesn't do it to this day, and it's been almost six months).

Two months ago we had a breakthrough: Mimei had an allergic reaction to a medication and became really sick. She wasn't able to walk properly kept falling down, and had considerable cardiovascular problems. So I drove her to the vet hospital.

During the anxious time in the waiting room I had time to think while the vets were taking care of Mimei. It was my fault and mine alone. Mimei needed a close bond now, a very close one, otherwise she would give up on herself. I saw that I had simply shut down emotionally – probably out of the feeling that I would have to give her up sooner or later, anyway. I loved her, but I was afraid to show it to her. She had done everything to get my attention. She even preferred to be scolded over being ignored. The poor animal.

While still in the waiting room, I decided that, no matter what would happen, Mimei would stay with us forever. This decision alone changed my entire feeling. Finally I allowed myself to love Mimei like our other dogs. Finally I opened up and was able to create a bond with Mimei. I felt better right away. But what about Mimei? It took another hour until the vet allowed me to come in. What he told me was astonishing: Mimei had almost died. She had to be resuscitated and nobody believed that she would make it. An hour and a half ago the dog suddenly regained her will to live (notice the times).

All of a sudden, she fought for her life and no longer let herself go. When I came to her with the vet Mimei was still weak, but crept towards me and buried her head in my arm.

She had never done that. Tears were streaming down my face.

What can I tell you: Mimei has completely recovered, she has not done anything naughty since and comes to me when I'm sitting at my computer to bury her head in my arm. She stays – and she wants to stay, no matter what happens. Our bond is very close now, and the "invisible lead" works most of the time.

So you see I'm only human, too, and like to escape into whining behaviour, like: "It's not my fault – the dog..."

When you read all the stories in here, you will recognize that each one started with a version of the whining and blaming behaviour. When we stop looking for the fault in others (that applies not only to dogs), our relationships become better and closer. We have to learn to allow our feelings and to show them. Only then can such a close bond and connection develop. How is it with you? Do you find the faults with your dog or with yourself? Are you able to love your dog unconditionally and without reservation? Or are your expectations such that you are disappointed every time when something doesn't work the way you envisioned it?

Unfortunately, I often hear: "I can't do this, the dog doesn't respond to me at all" and so on. Such statements mirror the whining behaviour like nothing else. "I can't" simply means: "I'm too lazy to work on it." "The dog doesn't respond to me" simply means: "This is work, I don't want to do this." "I have tried, but I simply can't do it" merely means: "Why should I spend more time working on it – it goes faster with force and traditional methods." (In that case I wonder seriously why this person came to me. Probably, because it didn't work.)

I admit, it is the hardest thing you can ask of people: rethinking, feeling and working on ourselves. Apart from that, it is so unbelievably difficult for us to criticize ourselves instead of others. It is work – 24 hours a day – it hurts, and it is terribly tiring at first. Especially when you have the courage to look at yourself in the mirror and not to blame other circumstances, previous histories, the environment, fate, and so on for your own mistakes. I know very well how hard it is and how difficult it is. But I also know how happy we are when we have succeeded, when we have a harmonious relationship with our dog (human, cat, hamster ...) that works always and everywhere and is satisfying like nothing else. This intimate connection that some people even manage to have with their human partner gives a security and a feeling of self worth that is simply indescribable – you feel invincible.

Make the decision right here and now to start with yourself and to build an incredible, phenomenal relationship with your environment, especially with your dog. Approach the exercises with enthusiasm and hang in there, no matter how hard it may be. What are a few weeks or even months of working on yourself, compared to a whole lifetime full of harmony and without problems?

You may like the little story that I found on the subject which follows.

The Wisdom of the Universe

A long time ago, the gods were thinking that it would be very bad if humans found the wisdom of the universe, before they were really ready for it. So the gods decided to hide the wisdom of the universe in a place where the humans wouldn't be able to find it until they were ready. One of the gods suggested hiding the wisdom on the highest mountain on earth. But the gods quickly realized that man would soon climb all the mountains and that the wisdom would not be hidden safely enough there. Another suggested hiding the wisdom in the deepest part of the ocean. But the gods saw the danger that mankind would find it there too soon as well. Then the wisest of the gods made his proposal: "I know what to do. Let's hide the wisdom of the universe in man himself. He will look for it there only when he is ready because he has to seek the path inside himself." The other gods were enthusiastic about this idea and thus hid the wisdom of the universe inside man himself.

(Anonymous)

The "Not" syndrome

Whenever I ask a new client what he expects of his dog, the first thing I hear is: "He must not ...; I don't want him to ...; he has to stop ....".

This is the "Not" Syndrome. We turn everything into negatives. When I keep asking, they say: "I want my dog to sit on command." – Fine, and why? "Because ... – dunno," ... So he doesn't ..." That's the "Not" Syndrome, too. And that is precisely human nature: being negative, just don't find anything positive – being a control freak is as much a part of it as the so-called collective consciousness: Everybody does it like that …

Ask anyone what their dog did a year ago that made him (the person) really happy. There is initially a long thoughtful silence and then, hours later, maybe an answer. But if you ask the question what the dog did a year ago that made him mad, you get an answer within seconds. So you see how much we are caught up in this negative thinking. Free yourself from it, think, feel and act positive. Write a "positive diary" in which you enter all the positive little things – learn to appreciate all the positive things and to ignore the negative. If you can do that you have climbed a few rungs on the ladder toward harmony.

Child and dog in harmony – free yourself of negative thoughts! (Photo: Tierfotoagentur.de/S. Schwerdtfeger)

Collective Consciousness

You, I, we are always aghast when we hear that an animal was tortured or abused somewhere. We almost go crazy when we read that a dog bit a child somewhere. We constantly read about the horrible conditions in foreign animal shelters and other horror stories. Are you aware that we are partially responsible for these conditions, by reading about them, being outraged by them, thinking about them? With each thought we feed the negative, so it continues to get worse.

A very good example is the so-called "fighting dog debate". There have always been so-called "fighting dog breeds", even long before our modern media existed. You didn't hear about incidents with these dogs in those days. Then a child was killed in Hamburg by a dog of that breed. The media reported in depth, you couldn't escape the sensationalist reports – the topic was discussed forever ad nauseam in all media outlets. Everybody, really everybody who was able to read, see, or hear, was informed about the incident. By watching and listening to this information, we fed the "morphic" (hypothetical) field "fighting dogs" with our psychological energy. What was the consequence? One incident involving dogs followed another. Since the media have quietened down about this subject, the "incidents" have become rarer in our consciousness again. Unfortunately, we now have such controversial breed laws on account of the irresponsible media coverage. Look around – you will find countless examples for this thesis – this reality.

The "Jack Sprat could eat no fat" aid

We all know the situation: We have been practising for days to be calm, positive and relaxed in any situation, and then it happens: our dog strolls away from us – runs towards a "danger". We want to start screaming hysterically – panic rises in us. Everything we learned is instantly forgotten. That happens to everybody sometimes. Then my daughter came up with the "Jack Sprat could eat no fat" aid. No, I'm not thinking of treats now – we don't need them. The "Jack Sprat could eat no fat" aid is for us humans, and you can't eat it, either: Write the following line on a wrist band: "Jack Sprat could eat no fat."

The wristband with the inscription helps you reduce tension and to regain the necessary calmness.

There are a lot of things in life that get on our nerves: the boss, the broken down car, the constant barking of our dog (for no reason, of course – why is the fleabag "jabbering" all the time ...), the whining of our partner (even worse than a barking dog) and so on. Our dogs are constantly aggravated as well: by the strange noise outside the door (hey, somebody is there, go look), when the owner delays the necessary walk (I have to go pee – come on!), when he is not allowed to play with his dog friend (Why can Hasso play and I have to stay with you?), by the wind in the trees (an odd sound, that makes me all fidgety), the mouse in the yard (What is that thing doing there?), by the holes he is not allowed to dig (Go ahead, enjoy your moles, then), by the good meat that he is not allowed to have (Eat it yourself, then!) and, and, and ...

Conversely, the aggravated dog aggravates us – a vicious cycle. And then you are supposed to focus on the bond and the "invisible lead"? Yes – especially then! Especially when we are all completely aggravated, we should sit down, pet our dog, take a deep breath, and stay calm. If that's too tiring, then blow off steam first. The punch bag helps us – a brisk walk helps your dog (brisk in the sense of brisk pace, not in the sense of "be back quickly"). The lazy ones among us do what I do when I don't feel like boxing: sit down quietly, count backwards slowly from 100 (well, sometimes from 1,000,000) and breathe deeply.

Whenever you are in a precarious situation, read the line aloud. You will see how that helps. You cannot say these words aloud and be in a panic at the same time – it simply doesn't work. As soon as you say this line, your breathing relaxes and you can think clearly again. Then take a deep breath and call your dog, relaxed – he will come. Try it! Please remember, there is only one way to success: do it!

Pure question of nerves

"The word discipline means learning, not controlling, submitting, imitating and adapting."

(Krishnamurti, Perfect Freedom)

Only bonding creates a connection

"Having feelings is to feel life and feeling life is to be alive."

(Anonymous)

You can understand your dog and his behaviour pretty well now, you give your dog confidence, security, and above all love. Then you also feel that there is a pretty close bond between you and your dog. Now you can start to let this bond grow into a connection. Remember, a bond – a connection – both have to grow, which takes time, patience, and – again – love. Take a look at the graphic depiction of how the transmission through vibrations, energy, and ultimately through thoughts, works.

The friendly thought

The dog feels the thought and the positive energy – he responds

The dog is there and the human goes crazy with joy

A Sign of Respect

In this context I want to say something about the topic "courtesy": courtesy is apparently no longer relevant in recent years. The words "thank you" and "please" pass the lips of certain individuals only very rarely and reluctantly. We should reintroduce this sign of respect – at least with our dogs.

When one of our own dogs has to do something for me, I say "please". When he has done it, I thank him for it. So I may sometimes say briefly: "Come, sit down", but in a very non-commanding tone of voice. Or I say: "Please sit down now ". When the dog sits, I don't lose anything by saying a friendly "thank you". Even if your dog doesn't understand the meaning of those words (which I don't believe) these phrases give them a different tone and psychologically there is true gratitude or true asking in you. In our seminars I often do a "mood test": first I greet the participants with a few brief words then I give them orders completely ignoring all politeness: "Sit down!", "get up!", "come here!"...

After half an hour in this tone of voice, I return to my normal voice and ask the participants how they felt during the first half hour. I don't have to write down the answers – everybody felt bad. As soon as you add the words "please" and "thank you", smile a little, make a joke, the entire mood changes drastically – everybody discusses and learns, happy and carefree. Why should we treat our dogs differently? They are more attentive and cooperative, when they are in a good and relaxed mood.

A practical example

Uwe, a passionate dog person in his fifties, came to us with his dachshund, Uzo, because he needed a few tips so that his Uzo would obey better outside. Uzo had the habit of not listening to any calls when he was busy with something. We went into our fenced play-yard first where Uwe took the dachshund off the lead. Initially, Uzo didn't dare to venture far away from his owner – he stayed within a radius of a few metres. Only when we added one of our own dogs Uzo became distracted, played with the other dog and romped around with him. Uwe called – not the slightest reaction from Uzo. It was only when his owner came into his field of vision that he came running over. We tried a few things and my initial suspicion hardened more and more: Uzo was almost deaf. We drove to our veterinarian who confirmed the diagnosis. At first, Uwe was shocked. He thought it was much too dangerous to let deaf Uzo off the lead. So the poor dog would only be able to run free in the little garden, Uwe complained. I taught him differently: two aids were necessary. A friend of ours invented one of them. The other one was the "invisible lead".

The invention was as simple as it was brilliant: a little device was attached to the harness, a kind of tiny hairbrush that vibrated by remote control. This brush was fastened to the harness so that the bristles faced towards the fur. Uwe held the transmitter, and when Uzo moved too far away, Uwe only pressed the button – the brush started vibrating very lightly and Uzo turned to look at his owner who could then indicate to him with hand signals and body language that he wanted him to come back. After a short time, this system worked very well. But in the house Uzo shouldn't have to wear the harness all the time. So we practised using the "invisible lead" with Uwe, just like you are doing now. After six months the two were able to communicate without words, just through gestures and body posture. Today, Uzo leads the life of a completely normal, happy dog – always in very close invisible contact with his beloved owner.

(Photo: Tierfotoagentur.de/J. Hutfluss)

You see, everything takes time – especially in this area nothing can be forced. The positive aspect of it is: We improve every day! The sooner you change your thinking and your actions, the sooner you get results. Some people can do it within a few days. Others need months.

Another example

The story happened a while ago. We always had countless dogs, some of them our own, some of them rescue cases, some of them boarded dogs. With so many dogs, our relationships with our own "house dogs" were often neglected. Especially my connection with our female Alaskan Malamute Ayumi Chan was not really optimal. We loved each other, no doubt, there was a close bond from the beginning (we got her from the breeder at eight weeks) – but there really was no connection. During her "storm and stress" age, Ayumi found her way outside one day. It was always her favourite hobby to roam through the woods and hunt mice. Now she was gone.

We fanned out to look for Ayumi. We had called all the hunters in the area on the phone for help. They all agreed to lookout for our "Grey". From time to time we received a phone call: "I saw your dog, but she didn't come. She ran away again immediately." Thus, we found out that she was roaming within a few kilometres' distance from our farm. But we couldn't see her anywhere – Ayumi had been gone for more than six hours now. She had never done that. Around 9 pm my daughter had had enough: "Focus and bring her here, instead of letting her run around the forest", she snapped.

Well, now I finally knew what it means to "forget yourself" … I went into the house, found a quiet place and focused on Ayumi. I pictured her running through our gate and asked her, very quietly, to finally come home. My husband stood watch by the gate – ten minutes later Ayumi came scurrying in, followed by our butcher's car. He had seen her suddenly racing out of the forest and running towards home, always nicely on the left side of the road. He stayed behind her with his car, so that nothing would happen to her – it was already completely dark. We all greeted our runaway emotionally and hugged her full of joy.

(Photo: Tierfotoagentur.de/S. Gervelis)

A final example

I had a special relationship with our shepherd-mix Luzifer from the very beginning. He is a son of Candy's, our therapy dog, born and raised on our farm. One day we were forced to part with Luzifer and Ayumi for a few months. They lived with a friend who was always in touch with us, while we were travelling "around the world". Sometimes we felt very bad – we missed the two. Our friend called regularly always at those times, in order to make us feel better. (Most of the time we were around 1,000 kilometres away from her.) How did she know that we were feeling bad? Very simple: Luzifer was agitated during those times and pooped in the house (which wasn't like him at all). When we were doing well, he was doing well, too, and acted friendly and happy.

Helpful tests

"How wonderful it is that nobody needs to wait even a single minute to start changing the world."

(Anne Frank)

Now we can begin together to change our little world. You have tossed aside everything that had been drilled into you? You know your dog, know that he is different, but not stupid or obtuse? You have the firm resolve to enter this mysterious bond that will soon make everybody else become green with envy? You are therefore ready to change your thinking, your actions and feelings? You have not only the will, but also the necessary sense of humour and self criticism to turn everything you have done up to now upside down? You are capable of ignoring the comments of others? You have forgotten everything that you had been taught?

Then you are ready for the following tests that show you what the bond looks like.

Bonding Test Part 1 – You bond with your dog

Answer the following questions honestly:

1. **If you used to own a dog who passed away, do you compare your present dog with him?**
   Yes (0 points) sometimes (5 points) no (10 points)

2. **Did you stay home with your dog for at least two weeks after you got him?**
   Yes (10 points) not continuously (5 points) no (0 points)

3. **Do you spend a certain amount of time exclusively and intensively with your dog (training doesn't count)?**
   Yes (10 points) sometimes (5 points) no (0 points)

4. **Are there certain rituals between you and your dog (listening to music together in the evenings, cuddling sessions, or other things)?**
   Yes (10 points) sometimes (5 points) no (0 points)

5. **Do you play with your dog when he comes to you, but you don't really feel like it?**
   Yes (10 points) sometimes (5 points) no (0 points)

6. **Does your dog come to you without being called when he is hurt?**
   Yes (10 points) sometimes (5 points) no (0 points))

7. **Have you ever taught your dog something "useless" just for fun (for example shaking hands, waving, closing doors, or something similar)?**
   Yes (10 points) sometimes (5 points) no (0 points)

8. **Do you show your dog clearly that you love him?**
   Yes (10 points) sometimes (5 points) no (0 points)

9. **When your dog wants to be scratched, do you do it often or rarely?**
   Most of the time (10 points) sometimes (5 points) never (0 points)

10. **Do you let your dog play as often as possible with other dog friends?**
    Yes (10 points) my dog has no friends (5 points) no (0 points)

11. **Do you know what your dog likes (food, toys, friends, humans)?**
    Yes (10 points) most of them (5 points) no, I'm often surprised (0 points)

12. **Do you tell your dog when you go away and when you will return approximately?**
    Yes (10 points) sometimes (5 points) no (0 points)

13. **Do you feel that your dog enriches your life?**
    Yes (10 points) sometimes (5 points) no (10 points)

Results

100 – 130 points:
Ideal

80 – 100 points:
You still have to work a little on yourself.

Fewer than 80 points:
You can't develop a bond this way – rethink everything quietly.

Bonding Test Part 2 – Your dog's bond with you

Answer the following questions honestly:

1. **Does your dog often follow your every move with his eyes?**
Yes (10 points) sometimes (5 points) no (0 points)

2. **Does your dog react properly when you only shake your head lightly at his request (food, owner?)?**
Yes (10 points) sometimes (5 points) no (0 points)

3. **Does your dog come to you when something scares him?**
Yes (0 points) sometimes (5 points) no (10 points)

4. **Can you touch your dog everywhere on his body without him flinching?**
Yes (10 points) sometimes (5 points) no (0 points)

5. **Does your dog always seek your presence (except when he is playing)?**
Yes (0 points) sometimes (5 points) no (10 points)

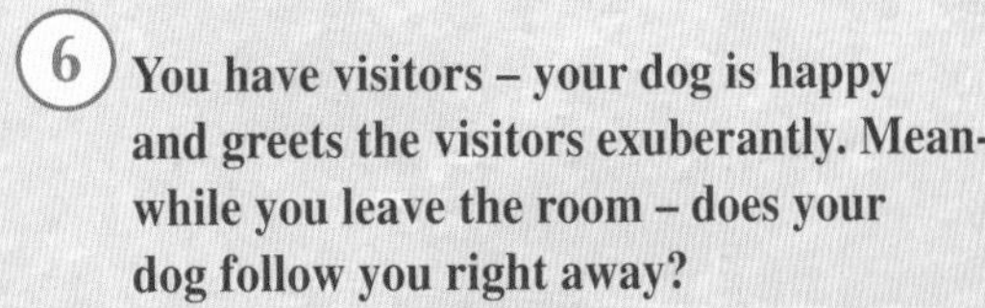

6. **You have visitors – your dog is happy and greets the visitors exuberantly. Meanwhile you leave the room – does your dog follow you right away?**
Yes (10 points) sometimes (5 points) no (0 points)

7. **You are lying on the sofa reading or watching TV – does your dog come to be petted?**
Yes (10 points) sometimes (5 points) no (0 points)

8. **You fall down and lie motionless on the ground. Does your dog come to you right away to check if you are OK?**
Yes (10 points) sometimes (5 points) no (0 points)

Results

Only when you can answer "yes" to all these questions without reservation is your dog's bond with you strong enough to continue with the exercises. If not, then there is still a little lack of trust – work on that first. If you have found that your bond really fits, you can start with the exercises for the "invisible lead".

Create an invisible lead

"Humans believe a lie that they have heard a hundred times much more easily than a truth that is completely new to them."

(Alfred Polgar)

A few words in advance: don't expect miracles, which doesn't mean that miracles don't occur – you have to adjust yourself and your thinking. This is hard work and takes time. The more you work on yourself, the faster there will be results. But: the more intensively you pressure yourself to

be successful the less you will succeed. Therefore: take it easy – then you make progress!

This is what the beginning looks like

Sit down somewhere in a comfortable place, let your dog do whatever he wants. Sit so that you can see him, but don't stare at him. If your dog is busy with something and is ignoring you, you start the exercise.

Look at your dog, think very lovingly of him, remember funny things that you both have experienced. Your dog will look at you shortly – do nothing but smile at him. Should he come to you, be happy, pet him, and let him go again. Repeat this exercise after one hour at the earliest – three times a day is enough at the beginning.

The second step

You sit down again, as quiet and relaxed as possible. Don't try to think of nothing – that doesn't work. Rather think of something pleasant. Perhaps your favourite melody helps, just loud enough that you can barely hear it with some difficulty. Let your dog do what he wants. If he comes to you, pet him briefly and let him go. The dog can also lie with you or by your feet, wherever he wants. Playing is not on the programme right now. If your dog won't relax, you play first, then you practise. You should both be relaxed – eliminate external interruptions as much as possible (turn off the phone and the doorbell).

Focus on your dog lovingly without interruption and observe him.

Are you quite comfortable? Good. Then focus on your dog – look at him quietly and lovingly, look at him very closely, as if you had to draw him later from memory. Memorize his features in detail. Sooner or later your dog will look at you – then look away. If he comes to you, pet him and let him go away again. When you have memorized him precisely, close your eyes and try to picture your dog exactly as you just observed him. Can you remember every one of his movements? No? Of course not, because you only focused on his outside. But you can certainly see him in your mind's eye now – can't you? If not, it doesn't matter (I'm not a visual type myself, either), but then you can feel him clearly – you know what he looks like and you could draw him precisely – if you were a visual type. Now you have mastered this task successfully. Take a break – relax the tension in you, relax the concentration.

This may all appear somewhat odd to you, don't worry, we won't get esoteric. The first exercises only serve to improve concentration. You can also meditate or do something else that trains your concentration. But if you do it this way, you will often feel that your dog suddenly becomes attentive, looks at you or even comes to you. Those are the first successes. Remember them well. It is ideal if you write everything down in detail – a kind of "positive diary" in which you only write down the successes. If something doesn't work the way you had envisioned it, you pick up this diary, read through your successes, and you will be positively surprised how fast everything works!

Pay attention to every little detail, every tiny little change in your relationship, in your dog's behaviour. Learn to see the successes! And remember:

"The essential is invisible to the eye."

(Antoine de Saint-Exupèry)

Feeling the dog – the third step

Now it gets a little more difficult. Sit down, close your eyes – do you know what your dog is doing at the moment? Is he looking at you, is he asleep, is he moving – how is he moving, is his tail moving, his eyes, his fangs? Is a foot twitching? Try to feel the dog with your eyes closed – from time to time you are allowed to look briefly, whether your feeling, your guess is correct. But then close your eyes again immediately and continue feeling …

You may use all your senses in this exercise, except your eyes. You can listen, you can smell, you may even touch, if your dog is close to you. After a while you can "eliminate" one sense at a time and you will know what your dog is doing at that moment. It can be that your dog responds to your exercises and comes to you. Don't send him away – scratch him and continue practising. Try to focus – direct all your senses (except your eyes) towards your dog.

Don't expect that this exercise will work right away. You should practise this briefly several times a day, no more than five minutes at a time. Sooner or later it will work and you will have built another piece of the "invisible lead". When it works you can soon do anything, and you will still know what your dog is doing at that moment. Then you are able to react early when there is a "danger". Even when you are talking to other people and your dog is a few yards away, you will always be partly focused on your dog. You feel when he moves too far away. (That won't happen any more when the "invisible lead" is completed, due to the thought connection.)

A practical example

We were walking in a dense forest with a small group: three people, three dogs. All dogs were off the lead and were snooping through the woods, approximately 50 yards away from us. Candy, my crossbred dog, is a passionate collector. She digs up anything that doesn't belong to the forest and brings it to me. Unfortunately, dead animals also belong in her collection, and I don't like that.

While we were hiking through the forest, I was explaining something to the group and we were quickly engrossed in the discussion. The dogs were spreading out somewhere in the undergrowth. Suddenly I just called: "Fie!" I felt that Candy wanted to pick something up that I didn't like. The others looked at me bewildered – what was wrong? Candy came and led us to the spot from which I had called her away – there were the remains of a dead rabbit …

Now, it's not like some "animal communicators" describe, that I tasted or smelled the carcass – yuck! No, I was still focused on Candy, although I was talking to the others. It was a feeling, an indistinct one. But since I know Candy very well, I knew how to interpret this feeling – and "Fie!" always fits in these situations with Candy. I didn't feel that she had found a carcass; it could have been something else disgusting. It is pure habit for me that a part of me is always focused on the dog. It doesn't even matter if it's my own dog or somebody else's.

With an unfamiliar dog I automatically look frequently, which many of my clients don't do with their own dogs, unfortunately. It is pure practice to be able to focus on more than one thing. When living with dogs it is an absolute necessity. "Invisible lead" or not – concentration on your dog is your first duty! The thought connection is, in a way, the ultimate perfection and makes things a lot easier later on. Then I can rely on my feeling, which tells me in time when something isn't right. Until then – practise concentrating.

Practical exercises to increase concentration and your own awareness

First exercise: Close your eyes and feel your dog as described above. At the same time, tap your right foot four times, then your left foot five times – always alternating. Practise this for three minutes. (You can set the alarm so that you don't have to focus on the time as well.). Do you still know what your dog is doing? Which limbs he is moving? Where and how he is lying? Is he panting? Is something twitching? Are his eyes open or closed?

Tip

If you have the option, keep a video camera rolling and record the movements of your dog. That way you can check more easily later on.

Second exercise: Just like the first exercise, but now you not only tap your feet, but you also recite this sentence: "Wherever you go – I go with you!"

It is pretty difficult to focus on so many things at the same time, isn't it? The more you repeat these exercises and the more you work on your ability to focus, the easier it will be for you. Please repeat all exercises, including the following ones, for an entire week patiently every day.

Third exercise: Now it gets a little easier. School your perception and attentiveness:

a) Take a walk with open eyes and ears. Pay attention to every little detail: to plants, small animals, other humans. Take in as many details as possible.

b) Pay closer attention to the body language of other people when you are talking to them. Observe the arm position, gestures, and facial expressions of other people.

c) Try consciously to distinguish between your interpretations and actual observations. You observe, for instance, that somebody is touching his nose and you think he is lying. Your observation was: he is touching his nose. Your interpretation: touching one's nose means lying. This interpretation can be accurate, but doesn't have to be.

d) Pay close attention during the next talk show on TV to the tone and the voices of the speakers. Be aware of the various voices and their characteristics.

e) Pay more attention to your own body language – do your gestures, facial expressions and posture fit your words and thoughts?

Have you done all the exercises? Regularly? Are you able to send out positive vibrations in your interactions with your dog? Are you in control of your feelings and thoughts? Then you will soon be able to lead your dog with your thoughts. If you want to understand what this all means and how this principle can affect your entire life, then read the next chapter: The Law of Attraction Principle for humans and the effects for the dog.

Last, but not least

The LOA principle

"Everything we are is a result of what we have thought.""

(Buddha)

This statement by the Buddha explains very simply what this is about and what I have explained and demonstrated on the previous pages: the LOA Principle.

LOA = Law of Attraction

This really means nothing other than that we create our entire world through our thinking. Remember the example of the "fighting dog debate" and its self-fulfilling prophecy! The origins of everything are our thoughts, and even more importantly, the feelings we send out.

Nothing reflects our feelings and emotions as clearly as a dog. The more you immerse yourself into the described exercises and the more you pay attention to what happens when and how, the more you will see how valid the LOA is. This applies to everything in your life, but here we are only concerned with you and your dog (For clarification see the graphics on page 68).

This is the reason for great misunderstandings. We simply often ignore very many vibrations from our environment. Certainly, you may have met a friend and noticed from a distance that he or she was unhappy or in a bad mood. You can sometimes feel it even without seeing or hearing the other person. Then you had one of those rare moments, in which you not only picked up on the vibrations of others, but you interpreted them correctly, too. If you think about it honestly: how often has it happened that you received negative vibrations (a colleague's envy, mobbing attempts, bad mood, sorrow and so on) – and how often has it happened that you have received positive vi-

The human is constantly emitting vibrations: positive ones, negative ones, neutral ones – usually he is not even aware of it. But the dog notices all vibrations – he cannot escape them. So the dog tries to respond. That is difficult for him, because our vibrations – you can call them moods, too – change all the time, often within fractions of a second. For the dog this is all hard to understand.

brations (joy, love, pure energy, joy of life)? – you see, we return again to negativity. We prefer to perceive negative things and sweepingly overlook the positive ones. Is it really surprising, then, that more negative things happen to us? Hardly.

When you see a house, do you see only its beauty or do you see immediately that the paint is peeling here, that the gutters are crooked there? Be honest! What about your dog? You notice right away when your dog doesn't execute a command or a request of yours. Do you notice, on the other hand, how often your dog does exactly what you want? Have you noticed that your dog is lying quietly and obediently on his blanket when you want to read? Did you notice yesterday that your dog came immediately when you called him? You didn't, did you? And here is the decisive factor:

The dog emits vibrations on a continual basis as well. We humans hardly notice them, unfortunately – it is as if we were stuck in a box that only allows minimal amounts to go through.

Every time you don't reward a positive behaviour of your dog, if you ignore it, but at the same time you confirm each negative behaviour immediately with negative, i.e. impatient, disappointed, angry vibrations, this negative behaviour will manifest.

LOA – with dogs

You call your dog and he doesn't come. You are annoyed, disappointed – these vibrations hit not just your dog, but also your own universe. The LOA, the law of attraction says:

You receive in multiples what you send out. In this case, it means: Your dog will not come to you right away the next time, either and – since you will emit negative vibrations again, he won't come immediately the following time, either. At some point, he won't come at all. You get exactly what you emit. Your behaviour comes back to you like a boomerang, and it always hits you on the head!

Conversely: your dog doesn't come when you first call. But you know the law now and you decide to send out a loving thought, together with your firm conviction that he will come immediately at the next call. You will see, he will come. Then we have positive vibrations, you are happy. The positive vibrations intensify – the boomerang comes back, this time with a positive charge, and it doesn't hit you on the head, but it brings you exactly what you want: your dog, everywhere and always.

LOA – This time without a dog

An example: I like to try out the LOA from time to time. During the weekly shopping in our village I often see a completely overloaded cashier. She tries really hard to be always friendly. But you can tell that she is stressed. The customers complain about the prices, the small grocery bags, and, and, and, ...

I usually joke around a little, but this time I wanted to find out for certain: she gave me a sum of £39.95 and I gave her two £20 notes and a £5 note. She counted the change and when she wanted to hand it to me, I told her to put it into the coffee jar. I said this because I really wanted to do something nice for her. At first, she was very surprised, then her face lit up and she wished me a great day – and this time it really came from her heart. I watched her for a little while and noticed how she was beaming at all the customers, and they all smiled back. Suddenly her job was fun – the customers, who used to be unfriendly or indifferent, looked at her as a person and were friendly. Why? Well, because now she was emitting an energy that she usually lacked. It was not the money I gave her – it was the recognition of her that I expressed that way. And, let's be honest, everybody can use that ...

And we are already back on the subject of dogs: our dog needs the feeling of recognition as well – over and over. In the very beginning of this book I told you how little our own dogs really have to do. I also said that outside our property our dogs have to come immediately when we call them. On

our property we don't really care. I know that my dogs come when I call them – outside the property. And because I know this and rely on it, they can't avoid these vibrations – the absorb them and respond positively: they come.

There is another example I want to share with you – it showed me how right our way is of helping not just the dog, but first of all the human and in doing so leading both towards a harmonious life:

Here is another graphic depiction of it: Everything you think and feel hits your dog with full force. If your feelings are positive, you get a positive reaction from your dog – if they are negative you get a negative reaction. Both will manifest in their own way. Therefore it's better just to emit positive feelings, which our dog more than deserves, right?

A practical example

It was one of those memorable encounters that happen once in a while in our life. We were on our way to the Baltic Sea with twelve dogs and took a break at a rest stop. I was walking three of our dogs on the lead across the grass behind the rest stop, when a dog came running towards us without a lead. A little behind him came a lady with a midsized crossbreed who was pulling on the lead like crazy. My dogs stayed on the lead, but I let them play a little with the dog that was running free. The lady with her crossbreed chided angrily: "How can somebody let a dog run free here – that's irresponsible!" Just at that moment a young man came calling his dog who promptly left our dogs and ran happily towards the young man.

The lady couldn't help giving the man a piece of her mind. He answered very calmly: "I always let Coda run free – she knows that she is not allowed near the cars and she has never got into an argument with another dog. She simply ignores aggressive dogs." I had to agree with him – the dog had circled my dogs cautiously at first and only approached after my three had invited her – the female completely ignored the mix and his lady. Man and dog went away – the lady stayed nearby.

We struck up a conversation and she told me that she had had problems with her Rudi from the beginning – he pulled on the lead, ran away, didn't come when she called – the usual ... The lady herself, Cora, was an extremely fearful type and negative to the bone. She saw dangers for herself and her

(Photo: Tierfotoagentur.de/M. Rohlf)

dog everywhere, was afraid that her car would break down (that's why she was at this rest stop, she took her car to an inspection every 500 kilometres), and, and, and ...

She told me more. She was a police officer by profession (that's what her father had wanted) and nobody liked her, not her colleagues and her "customers" even less. She was so hardened and frustrated that I felt sorry for both of them – the dog and Cora.

We had a very long talk and of course we also spoke about the young man with his female dog. I explained to her that such behaviour was a little too risky for me, but that I could understand why nothing happened to the dog. I explained our approach and the LOA to her. Of course she didn't believe a word. But we exchanged phone numbers and agreed to meet on the Baltic Sea shore. Then we went our separate ways.

Close to our destination – the Island of Fehmarn – we took another break at the last rest stop. There we met Cora again – her car had broken down for a lack of oil. It would not have been a big deal. Fill up the oil, done. But no, Cora had to sleep in her car, so that everything could be checked by a mechanic the next morning. I explained to her that a gas station attendant or a trucker could check something like that as well.

She gathered up all her courage and went into the gas station. The attendant brushed her off rudely, he had no time. I saw a trucker standing at the counter, approached him with a friendly attitude and described Cora's problem to him. He immediately went, got his tools and took a look at Cora's car. He found that she must have forgotten to fill up the oil and went on his way. Cora was astonished: Nobody had ever done something like that for her. I explained the old saying to her: "Whatever you shout into the forest comes back as the echo." Now she understood. Cora followed on behind us until Fehmarn and she was therefore sure that nothing could happen.

During our days on the island, I really had time to explain the LOA to Cora and to do several test runs with her. At the end I gave her the advice to respond to her mobbing colleagues with an honest smile, to ignore anything negative and to focus only on the positive – no matter how insignificant.

Half a year later Cora attended one of our seminars: how much she had changed. She was happy – her dog was calm and obedient. Later she told me she had initially found it very difficult, but then she looked at her wristband every time a negative thought arose, and read the inscription aloud: "Jack Sprat could eat no fat." The colleagues had looked at her strangely, but they had to laugh, too. Slowly, but surely, her relationship with her colleagues had become more relaxed, and as a result her private life and her relationship with her dog had changed as well. Her joyfulness was infectious, not just for herself, but also for her colleagues – the positive vibrations had multiplied and were returning to her. The negative ones were replaced more and more. She showed me her thick positive diary: The beginning contained the entries of several days on one page. But soon the entries of a single day filled several pages ... When something went wrong for Cora, she was briefly annoyed, wrote the event off and forgot about it. She was looking for solutions – not for problems. Oh, and Cora left her job with the police department and is now working as a freelance dog trainer, for the canine police unit, among others.

Result? Feel good and nothing, absolutely nothing, can throw you off.

Important

You cannot lie to your dog or the universe. If your feelings and thoughts are not honestly positive deep down inside, then it usually doesn't work. Therefore, work intensively on yourself first, then everything else will come by itself. Try it out!

NLP – Neurolinguistic Programming

Want some science? The *"Network Science of Success"* writes about the experiences with the LOA in the area of health care in a press release (2008): "Could it be – we want more health – but we create more sickness?"

A brief comment regarding the understanding of the "law of attraction". The realization that our thoughts have a great impact on our life is nothing new to mental trainers. This law is based on the assumption that equals attract, that human thoughts act like magnets, so that in our life more of the things happen that we focus our attention on.

If somebody had met a Bill Gates 50 years ago and had heard of his visions, they probably would have written him off as a "weirdo". Now everybody around the world communicates with everyone else – one of his visions has almost become a reality today. Somehow we typically seem to meet innovators and consequently all innovations in three stages. First they are considered "pie in the sky". In the next stage, one wonders whether "there is something to it", after all, and finally, in stage three, a "medal" is awarded for it.

You see, the existence of the LOA can no longer be denied. Countless books have been written on the subject. Motivational coaches use the LOA, mental trainers, without whom nothing happens in sports any more, spread it.

NLP (Neurolinguistic Programming) uses the LOA as well. Until a few years ago, access to NLP was limited mostly to corporate managers. NLP is the so-called "new psychology". It is above all about communication techniques, but also about recognizing and underscoring the positive in one's own life as well as in the lives of others. NLP is really a way of learning the LOA for oneself.

What exactly is Neurolinguistic Programming?

- NLP is the study of how we literally "construct" our life through our mental models, our thoughts and ideas.
- NLP is the study of how "beliefs" and "perceptions" work in us and in all other beings.
- NLP is a collection of abilities to gain control over one's own mental processes.
- The term Neurolinguistic Programming is composed of:
  - Neuro – the neurological system: How sensory perceptions are translated into images and thoughts, consciously and subconsciously.
  - Linguistic – the language: How we use language and how we communicate with ourselves (internally) and with others

(externally), the totality of communication (including body language).

- Programming – the patterns, the processes, the structures: Which internal and external processes we use and how we can recognize and change them specifically.

To sum up: LOA is the Law of Attraction and NLP is the method of bringing about the changes in oneself and in others.

So you see, neither LOA nor NLP are pie in the sky – they are a simple method of shaping one's life in a positive way and – in our case – to build a completely harmonious relationship with our dog that can stand up to all resistances. And that is, after all, what we want. That's how we all get our "Lassies" and "Rexes", and without drilling or bribes – basically completely effortlessly ...

And another piece of advice from me: it is not modern to show feelings. But if you do it anyway, your world changes – for the better. You have read it several times that I'm an emotional person – my animals thank me every day – and I don't care what others think.

Do it like the sundial – only count the sunny hours!

Appendix

The author

Born in the USA, Angie Mienk is a German citizen, and took turns growing up in the USA and in Germany. Her grandfather and father were highly successful dog trainers for customs, police, and the US Army. There were always at least two family dogs and one or two training dogs in the house.

In the US, Angie Mienk studied veterinary medicine for two semesters, then human psychology (she graduated in this area with a PhD in 2007 in the US) and animal psychology (animal psychology is a recognized profession in the USA, that requires a complete university curriculum). She simultaneously studied to become a professional dog trainer at a large kennel.

Back in Germany, Angie Mienk turned her hobby into her profession. Because of her involvement with sometimes more than 60 dogs at a time that supposedly had behavioural issues, she studied the LOA principle and NLP (that had hitherto existed only for humans) and adapted it for dogs and their humans. Ever since she teaches the gentle and harmonious interaction with dogs according to these principles – more than 1,000 dogs worldwide are grateful to her.

Today several dogs live with Angie Mienk and her family. All of them periodically demonstrate on video and regularly at seminars how simple life can be. Her motto: there are only four letters for success: DO IT!

The author's homepage is www.hundeguru.com and she runs courses and seminars in both German and English.

Recommended literature

Coppinger, Ray
Dogs: a Startling New Understanding of Canine Origin, Behavior and Evolution
Prentice-Hall, 2001

Dahl, Dorothee
Good Times with Older Dogs: Care, Fitness and Health
Cadmos, 2009

Fisher, Sarah and Miller, Marie
100 Ways to Train the Perfect Dog
David & Charles, 2008

Fogle, Bruce
RSPCA New Complete Dog Training Manual
Dorling Kindersley, 2006

Gutmann, Monika
Line Training for Dogs: How it's Done
Cadmos, 2009

Mielke, Kerstin
Anatomy of the Dog: In Straightforward Terms
Cadmos, 2010

Sondermann, Christina
Playtime for Your Dog: Keep Him Busy Throughout the Day
Cadmos, 2006

Thank You

I owe a debt of gratitude to all my former bosses and former teachers, who all made sure that I never had time to follow the current trends of dog training, or even to find out about them. I want to thank especially all four-legged teachers who kept showing me how to lead a harmonious life with animals, even if their history didn't make it seem likely.

I also want to thank all those people who put stumbling blocks in my path, because they made me strong – and thank you to the animals and humans who supported me. Thank you to my clients who go the path of harmony with us. I owe a debt of gratitude to many more humans and animals – I thank them every morning before getting up – we are connected in thought.

A special Thank you is due to my exceedingly patient and cooperative editor, Ms. Poppe, as well as the CEO of Cadmos Books, Mr. Schmidtke.

CADMOS Books

Martina Nau

Snooping Around!

This book contains a wealth of ideas on how everybody can keep their dogs busy and entertained with games all around their sense of smell. The tasks and games described here will entertain both the human and their dog, challenging and employing a dog's instincts, and will ultimately strengthen the relationship between us and our dog companions.

80 pages, full colour, Softcover
ISBN 978-0-85788-200-4

Christina Sondermann

Playtime For Your Dog

This book will help you discover and employ games and activities on an everyday basis that both you and your dog will enjoy and that will contribute towards his fitness and training: Marvel at the super-abilities of your dog's sense of smell. Make his daily walks an exciting adventure. Find enough inspiration in your living room to exercise his basic play instincts. With step-by-step illustrations.

128 pages, full colour, Hardcover
ISBN 978-3-86127-922-8

Anders Hallgren

Mental Activation

Dogs need to encounter and overcome physical and mental challenges to remain stimulated, happy and well. Anders Hallgren describes many simple exercises designed to engage and improve a dog's senses. 'A wealth of fun ideas for increasing the interaction between you and your dog' – Your Dog.

96 pages, full colour, Softcover
ISBN 978-3-86127-927-3

Dagmar Cutka

Safe and Sound with Child and Dog

This practical guide highlights the criteria you should be aware of when choosing your future family dog, it gives tips on family dog training and advice on how best to prepare a dog already living in a household for the arrival of a new baby. Play-based educational games, practical experience, together with many photos make this book an indispensable companion.

80 pages, full colour, Softcover
ISBN 978-3-86127-971-6

Kerstin Mielke

Anatomy of the Dog

If you want to find out more about how your dog's body works and functions, you will find detailed information here in this book. Special emphasis is placed on movement and locomotion as these are of particular importance to all dogs. The inner organs, skin and coat, nervous system and senses and their physiology are also described in detail. Several detailed drawings help explain each area of the anatomy of the dog.

96 pages, full colour, Softcover
ISBN 978-3-86127-979-2

For more information, please visit: www.cadmos.co.uk CADMOS